SPEAK LIFE

TO YOUR

DREAMS

FRANK SANTORA

Frank Santora Ministries
600 Danbury Road
New Milford, CT 06776
www.franksantora.cc

ISBN: 9781976927218
Printed in the United States of America
©2018 by Frank Santora
All rights reserved.

Unless otherwise noted, Scripture is taken from the New King James Version. Copyright ©1982 by Thomas Nelson, Inc. Used by permission. All rights reserved.

No part of this book may be reproduced or transmitted in any form or by any means, electronic or mechanical, including photocopying, recording or by any information storage and retrieval system, without permission in writing from the author.

Ezekiel 37:1-14

The hand of the Lord came upon me and brought me out in the Spirit of the Lord, and set me down in the midst of the valley; and it was full of bones. Then He caused me to pass by them all around, and behold, there were very many in the open valley; and indeed they were very dry. And He said to me, "Son of man, can these bones live?" So I answered, "O Lord God, You know." Again He said to me, "Prophesy to these bones, and say to them, 'O dry bones, hear the word of the Lord! Thus says the Lord God to these bones: "Surely I will cause breath to enter into you, and you shall live. I will put sinews on you and bring flesh upon you, cover you with skin and put breath in you; and you shall live. Then you shall know that I am the Lord."'" So I prophesied as I was commanded; and as I prophesied, there was a noise, and suddenly a rattling; and the bones came together, bone to bone. Indeed, as I looked, the sinews and the flesh came upon them, and the skin covered them over; but there was no breath in them. Also He said to me, "Prophesy to the breath, prophesy, son of man, and say to the breath, 'Thus says the Lord God: "Come from the four winds, O breath, and breathe *on these slain, that they may live."'" So I prophesied as He commanded me, and breath came into them, and they lived, and stood upon their feet, an exceedingly great army. Then He said to me, "Son of man, these bones are the whole house of Israel. They indeed say, 'Our bones are dry, our hope is lost, and we ourselves are cut off!' Therefore prophesy and say to them, 'Thus says the Lord God: "Behold, O My people, I will open your graves and cause you to come up from your graves, and bring you into the land of Israel. Then you shall know that I am the Lord, when I have opened your graves, O My people, and brought you up from your graves. I will put My Spirit in you, and you shall live, and I will place you in your own land. Then you shall know that I, the Lord, have spoken it and performed it," says the Lord.'"*

INTRODUCTION

Every year around January 1st, it seems the whole world gets geared up making New Year's Resolutions, in yet another attempt to use will-power and self-discipline to break bad habits, turn around financial situations, and repair broken relationships. But did you know that, as a child of God, He promises you so much more than just 'hopeful resolutions' to change habits and circumstances? And you don't have to wait till January to begin to turn your circumstances around; you can start your 'new year' today, right now! In fact, as a child of God, He has given you the authority to prophetically declare that starting this very moment, this year will be your Banner Year!

...not by might nor by power, but by my Spirit, says the Lord...

It's true! Starting right now, this can be your year of good breaks, when the tide turns and moves in your favor; your year of financial increase and blessing; your year of spiritual growth, seeing answered prayers and God showing up in miracles! This can be your year of restored health, freedom from addiction, and restoration of family harmony, unity and love.

This year can be your year of God opportunities, and your year of return, when everything lost or stolen by the enemy in the past must be returned seven-fold! It can be your year of release, where everything that has kept you in bondage loses its grip on you forever. And this year can be your year of restoration, where everything broken or damaged in your life gets put back, and repaired to better than it's ever been.

It's your banner year... if you want it.

In the pages that follow, I want to give you seven principles concerning the personal prophetic declarations you will need to make over your life that are absolutely necessary for you to experience your banner year!

As we come to the text in Ezekiel, the nation of Israel is going through a period of time where they have become fragmented, scattered and spiritually dismembered. They have become captive to their natural enemies and have lived that way long enough to produce a sense of hopelessness in them. Their plight is depicted by God to Ezekiel in a vision where he is walking through a valley of dry bones, or more literally, a graveyard full of corpses.

This is the picture God paints of Israel's condition at that time, but it is also a vivid picture of what life circumstances have done to many people today. Hurtful events have fragmented them, scattered them, dismembered them... fragmented their families, scattered their hopes, dismembered their dreams. And as they walk through life, they are surrounded by their own dead corpses and dry bones.

The dry bones of...

- sad memories
- lost opportunities
- a failed marriage and bitter divorce
- the loss of a loved one
- being taking advantage of
- emotional or physical abuse
- addictive behavior
- financial struggle
- lost peace
- the absence of joy

And even, the dry bones of hopelessness.

In just this situation, God makes a big promise to the nation of Israel. He is going to gather them, put them back together, unify them and bring them back to their own land. In the same way, God has given you the promise that this can be your year of Jubilee, of being set free and restored to fullness and blessing in every area of your life.

But along with the promise, God gives them, and us, a strategy to accomplish this restoration. What is the strategy? Simply this... open your mouth and speak. Prophesy to those dry bones!

Listen to me, child of God! If this year is going to be your banner year, you'd better start prophesying to your dry bones. Speak to the dry bones of circumstances and relationships in your life and command them to live. Command the breath of life to come into them by the words of your mouth.

Be bold! Tell them to get up, to stand up! Tell sinews to connect to the bones.

Tell muscles to connect to the bones. Tell flesh to cover the bones. Tell breath to enter the bones. Tell the bones to march... and tell them to come home.

Prophesy to them bones!

Start by speaking to your mind, to agree with and believe the word of God. Speak to your finances to prosper and grow. Speak life to your kids. Speak restoration to your health. Speak love and respect to your marriage. Speak favor and promotion to your job. Speak healing to your hurts, pains and scars.

It's time to prophesy to your dead bones, your dead hopes and dreams, and say, "get up and live again, 'cause this is my banner year"!

Scripture tells us over and over that our words are one of the single most powerful influencers of the life we live. Our words can call forth death or life, curses or blessings, to manifest in our lives.

> *Death and life are in the power of the tongue, and those who love it will eat its fruit.*
> **Proverbs 18:21**

Our words can keep us bound...

> *You are snared by the words of your mouth; you are taken by the words of your mouth.*
> **Proverbs 6:2**

or our words can bring us freedom.

> *For by your words you will be justified, and by your words you will be condemned.*
> **Matthew 12:37**

The Book of James puts it like this... Your words are the steering wheel to your life!

> *If anyone does not stumble in word, he is a perfect man, able also to bridle the whole body. Indeed, we put bits in horses' mouths that they may obey us, and we turn their whole body. Look also at ships: although they are so large and are driven by fierce winds, they are turned by a very small rudder wherever the pilot desires. Even so the tongue is a little member and boasts great things.*
> **James 3:2-5**

Here is what God is saying. If you want your life to go in a different direction, you've got to steer it in that direction. You do that by the words that come out of your mouth.

Don't believe me, or do you think that is an exaggeration? Listen to the words of Jesus:

> *So Jesus answered and said to them, "Have faith in God. For assuredly, I say to you, whoever says to this*

> mountain, 'Be removed and be cast into the sea,' and does not doubt in his heart, but believes that those things he says will be done, he will have whatever he says. Therefore I say to you, whatever things you ask when you pray, believe that you receive them, and you will have them."
> **Mark 11:22-24**

I call that the WYSIWYG principle: **W**hat **Y**ou **S**ay **I**s **W**hat **Y**ou **G**et!

So, son of man, prophesy to these dry bones. Speak life to your circumstances, situations, marriage, health, job, relationships, career, dreams, finances or whatever else has become a pile of dead bones in your life.

As we look closer at our text, there are Seven Principles of Prophetic Declaration that God gives to Ezekiel that I'm challenging you to practice, to make this year, your victorious Banner Year!

PRINCIPLE ONE
Nothing happens until you speak

I love the fact that the text begins with "The hand of the Lord came upon me and brought me out in the Spirit of the Lord."

The hand of the Lord was on me.

You can interpret that to mean...the hand of favor and power was upon me. The hand that touched the eyes of the blind and made them see, was on me. The hand that touched the skin of the lepers and healed them... the hand that formed man and women from the dust of the ground... the hand that cast out demons and put the devil on the run... the hand that restores, saves and sets free... WAS ON ME.

God was all over me; His power was running through me, ready to operate for me, and yet He simply said to me, "prophesy to these dry bones."

These are the kinds of things that make you say, hmmm...'Why God? 'Cause, if you promised it, and You will it, then why don't You just make it happen?' But God's response is, 'The way I want to make it happen is when you speak out in faith what I tell you; nothing in your life is going to change or move until *you tell it to*.'

...Let the redeemed of the Lord say so!
Psalms 107:2

It doesn't say, let the redeemed of the Lord...

- think so
- hope so
- wish so
- or even pray so

It says, "Let the redeemed of the Lord **say** so"! Say to your marriage, it's time for you to be blessed. Say to your finances, it's time for you to start to overflow. Say to your kids, it's time for you to live for God. Say to your dreams, it's time for you to come to pass. Say to your joy, it's time for you to return to my life. Say to your pain, it's time for you to be healed.

Let the redeemed of the Lord say so, because nothing changes in your life until you say it is so!

Remember, the earth didn't come into being till God said so. Lazarus didn't come out of his tomb till Jesus said so. The woman with the issue of blood didn't get healed till she said so. Blind Bartimaeus didn't start seeing till he said so. David didn't defeat Goliath till he said so. Shadrach, Meshach and Abednego didn't get saved in the fiery furnace till they said so. Daniel didn't come out of the lion's den alive till he said so. The man at the gate called Beautiful didn't get healed, till Peter and John said so.

And nothing moves in your life, till you say so.

Let the redeemed of the Lord say so!

PRINCIPLE TWO
Speak what God says about your situation

Now some people get off in a ditch with this principle of declaration. They say all sorts of crazy things. They say things like, 'I'm tall, dark and handsome', even though they are short and fair-skinned. They say things like, 'God's going to put a million dollars in my mailbox.' They say things like, 'I can sing like Whitney Houston,' even though they can't carry a tune in a bucket.

They think this principle means to say whatever you want and get whatever you desire. But that's not what the principle is about.

Let's look again at our text:

> *And He said to me, "Son of man, can these bones live?" So I answered, "O Lord God, You know." Again He said to me, "Prophesy to these bones, and say to them, 'O dry bones, hear the word of the Lord! Thus says the Lord God to these bones: "Surely I will cause breath to enter into you, and you shall live. I will put sinews on you and bring flesh upon you, cover you with skin and put breath in you; and you shall live. Then you shall know that I am the Lord.""'*
> **Ezekiel 37: 3-6**

Ezekiel spoke what God told him to say, and that's why it worked. You see, the key to having a banner year is declaring what God says about you and your situation, in His word.

The Scripture says in Hebrews 10:23:

> *Let us hold fast the confession of our hope without wavering, for He who promised is faithful.*

The word confession here is the Greek word 'homologian'. 'Homo' means same; 'logian' means words. When you put them together, it means to say the same thing as God says. Not just saying anything you desire about your situation, but saying what God says about your situation!

And check this out. You must hold fast to it, and don't waiver from it. That means find out what God says about you and your situation and speak that over your life continually, no matter how foolish it seems, and no matter who tries to talk you out of it.

So, you may not be able to say you are tall, dark and handsome, but you can say:

> *For we are His workmanship, created in Christ Jesus for good works, which God prepared beforehand that we should walk in them.*
> **Ephesians 2:10**

and

> *Beloved, now we are children of God; and it has not yet been revealed what we shall be, but we know that when He is revealed, we shall be like Him, for we shall see Him as He is.*
> **1 John 3:2**

You may not be able to say God is going to drop a million bucks in your mailbox, but you can say:

> *The Lord your God will make you abound in all the work of your hand, in the fruit of your body, in the increase of your livestock, and in the produce of your land for good. For the Lord will again rejoice over you for good as He rejoiced over your fathers...*
> **Deuteronomy 30:9**

and

> *Let them shout for joy and be glad, Who favor my righteous cause; And let them say continually, "Let the Lord be magnified, Who has pleasure in the prosperity of His servant."*
> **Psalms 35:27**

You may not be able to say you have a singing voice like Whitney Houston, but you can say:

> *Having then gifts differing according to the grace that is given to us, let us use them: if prophecy, let us prophesy in proportion to our faith.*
> **Romans 12:6**

You may not be able to say you will live a problem-free life, but you can say:

> *But the path of the just is like the shining sun, that shines ever brighter unto the perfect day.*
> **Proverbs 4:18**

and

> "No weapon formed against you shall prosper, and every tongue which rises against you in judgment, you shall condemn. This is the heritage of the servants of the Lord, and their righteousness is from Me," says the Lord.
> **Isaiah 54:17**

You can say anything which is promised you in God's Word, like:

- I am getting stronger, healthier and wiser
- My youth is being renewed like the eagles
- I will live long and see the salvation of the Lord
- I am blessed and prosperous
- I am strong and confident
- I am creative
- I am secure
- I am well-liked

- The right people are in my future
- I will overcome every obstacle
- I am valuable, one of a kind
- I have royal blood flowing through my veins
- I wear a crown of favor
- I am a child of the most-high God
- I am excelling
- I am forgiven and free
- I am redeemed
- I wear a robe of righteousness
- God is well-pleased with me
- I am increasing in anointing, wisdom, favor and influence
- This is my banner year...my year of victory!

Say what God says about your situation, and watch your dry bones live!

PRINCIPLE THREE
Speak up when you are tempted to shut up
&
Shut up when you are tempted to speak up

Notice the question God asks Ezekiel. Ezekiel is standing in the middle of a graveyard, and God says, "Can these dry bones live?" Ezekiel's response: "Only you know, God."

Translation ... *umm, I'm not really sure.*

I'm not really sure God, that if I speak to these dry bones, they will come back to life. And I'm not really sure God, that if I speak over my marriage, it will be restored, because You know, the love there is dead...I'm not really sure God, that if I speak over my body it will be healed...the doctors said some scary things. And I'm not really sure God, that if I speak over my finances, I will have more than enough, 'cause I've got more month than money. I'm not really sure God, that if I speak over my pain it will go away. I've carried it for so long now, it's become a part of me.

God, you mean to tell me that if I start speaking over my life, it's all just going to change? Why, that's laughable.

If that's what you are thinking now, God's got a word for you...*You must speak up when you are tempted to shut up.*

Jesus walked into the home of a man named Jairus, whose daughter was dead, and He said to her:

> *"Little girl, arise." Then her spirit returned, and she arose immediately.*
> **Luke 8:55-56**

During a three year drought in Israel, the prophet Elijah called an end to it, telling his servant:

> "Go up, say to Ahab, 'Prepare your chariot, and go down before the rain stops you.'" Now it happened in the meantime that the sky became black with clouds and wind, and there was a heavy rain.
> **1 Kings 18:44-45**

David looked square in the face of a ten foot giant, holding only a sling shot and five smooth stones and said:

> "This day the LORD will deliver you into my hand, and I will strike you and take your head from you..." Then David put his hand in his bag and took out a stone; and he slung it and struck the Philistine in his forehead, so that the stone sank into his forehead, and he fell on his face to the earth...David ran and stood over the Philistine, took his sword and

drew it out of its sheath and killed him, and cut off his head with it.
1 Samuel 17:46, 49, 51

Shadrach, Meshach and Abednego looked at a wicked king and a fiery furnace, and said:

"… our God whom we serve is able to deliver us from the burning fiery furnace, and He will deliver us from your hand, O king".... Then these men were bound in their coats, their trousers, their turbans, and their other garments, and were cast into the midst of the burning fiery furnace....Then Nebuchadnezzar went near the mouth of the burning fiery furnace and spoke, saying, "Shadrach, Meshach, and Abednego, servants of the Most High God, come out, and come here." Then Shadrach, Meshach, and Abednego came from the midst of the fire.
Daniel 3:17, 21, 26

And Ezekiel looked at a graveyard full of dead bones and said, 'Dry bones live!'

All these things were laughable declarations in the face of circumstances that seemed like they couldn't change by simply speaking a few words. In every example above, there was the very real temptation to shut up, because it seemed foolish to declare such things in the face of such circumstances. Can't you just hear the little voice going off in their heads, saying, "This is stupid! Speaking to this situation is not going to change it, so just shut up!"

I like what our text in Ezekiel says in verse 7 and 10:

"So I prophesied as I was commanded..."

Can't you just hear the prophet testifying later: I had my doubts about it... it didn't make sense in my head... I couldn't understand how my words could change my circumstances. I felt foolish and others laughed at me, but I spoke up, even though I was tempted to shut up, and I saw in those dry bones the impossible happen! Those dry bones came to life!

Child of God, I know it seems stupid! I know at times you can feel foolish, speaking about:

- your loveless, sexless, no communication marriage, as though it was heaven on earth
- your finances, as though you don't have a financial care in the world
- your health, as though you don't have to go through chemo
- your job, as though you have favor and promotion on the way
- your kids, as if they are on fire for God
- your dreams, as though they are coming to pass quickly

- your pain, as though it's a thing of the past

Others may even talk about you, but do as you have been commanded by your heavenly Father. Speak up when you are tempted to shut up. Declare what God says about your situation even if it doesn't look that way... even if it seems ridiculous.

As children, we are supposed to copy the way our Daddy talks, and that's how God does it.

> God, who gives life to the dead and calls into being that which does not exist...
> **Romans 4:17 (AMP)**

What that means is, declare what God says about your situation even if it doesn't look that way, and **especially** if it doesn't look that way! Speak up when you are tempted to shut up and watch your dry bones (your dead circumstances), come alive in your life.

And just as important... shut up when you are tempted to speak up!

There are two things that happen when we are going through a challenging situation: we are tempted to shut up when it comes to declaring what God says about our circumstances when our circumstances don't look like God says... and we are tempted to speak up and talk about how bad the circumstances look.

Can anybody relate?

Our temptation when we are going through a tough time is to keep talking about how tough the time is and how bad the circumstances are. Some people will say, 'well that's just reality.'

No, that's just stupidity.

That's just taking the bait of Satan, and it will stop you from tapping into one of the most powerful weapons God has given to us to change our circumstances... declaring not what our situation is, but what our situation will be!

So when you are tempted to complain, talk about the problem, reiterate what 'is' time after time, tell everybody around you what's really going on, and commiserate with anyone who will listen... then it's time to SHUT UP!

Come on somebody, that's how you see your dry bones live!

PRINCIPLE FOUR
Speak *to* your dry bones, not *about* your dry bones

This is so important! Look at what God says to Ezekiel:

> *Again He said to me, "Prophesy to these bones..."*

Prophesy to, speak to... not, speak about.

Remember the words of Jesus in Mark 11:23: *For assuredly, I say to you, whoever says to this mountain, 'Be removed and be cast into the sea,' and does not doubt in his heart, but believes that those things he says will be done, he will have whatever he says.*

Jesus, the living Word of God, says to you, 'speak **to** the mountain'... and speak **to** your dry bones!

That's the rub, isn't it? That's the struggle. It's a whole lot easier to talk about the mountain.

- How big it is
- How difficult it is
- How hopeless it looks
- How long it's been there
- How it makes you feel
- What it's doing to you inside
- How it has robbed you in life

We're really good at being reporters, relating exactly how things are. But listen to me, child of God! God has not commanded us to be reporters; He's commanded us to be forecasters!

There is this amazing scripture in Zechariah 4:7, about a man named Zerubbabel, who was one of the leaders of the tribe of Judah, and whose 'mountain' was to lead Israel out of Babylonian captivity. Now, that's a big mountain.

But look at what Zerubbabel did!

'So, big mountain, who do you think you are? Next to Zerubbabel you're nothing but a molehill.'
Zechariah 4:7 (MSG)

And guess what, it happened! He led Israel out. God has not called us to be reporters about how big and bad our mountain is. He has called us to be forecasters about our future, declaring what He says about us and our circumstances.

Don't speak about your mountain... speak to your mountain! Don't speak about the dry bones, Ezekiel. Speak to the dry bones!

PRINCIPLE FIVE
Speak to your mountain about your God

Now here is where these principles get really powerful. Did you notice what Ezekiel said to the dry bones? It's a declaration about what God is going to do... how big He is, and how powerful.

> Thus says the Lord God to these bones: "Surely I will cause breath to enter into you, and you shall live. I will put sinews on you and bring flesh upon you, cover you with skin and put breath in you; and you shall live. Then you shall know that I am the Lord."
> **Ezekiel 37:5-6**

Many of the great Bible victories came to pass in people lives because they didn't just speak to their mountains, they spoke to their mountain about their God.

David said to his mountain, the giant warrior Goliath, "the LORD will deliver you into my hand."

Shadrach, Meshach and Abednego said to their mountain, King Nebuchadnezzar, "…our God whom we serve is able to deliver us from the burning fiery furnace."

Peter and John said to their mountain, a paralyzed beggar, "silver and gold I do not have, but what I do have I give you: In the name of Jesus Christ of Nazareth, rise up and walk."

And Ezekiel looked at a graveyard full of dead bones and prophesied in the name of the Lord, 'Dry bones live!'

No matter how big your mountain is, how bad your mountain has become, or how insurmountable your mountain appears, begin to declare to your mountain how big your God is and watch it become a molehill. Declare what the Word says about God:

- Sickness, my God is a healer!
- Finances, my God is a provider!
- Marriage, my God is a mender!
- Wayward child, my God is a way-maker!
- Heart break, my God is a comforter!
- Anxiety, my God is a peace-giver!
- Confusion, my God is full of wisdom!
- Buried dreams, my God is resurrection!
- Misfortune, my God is full of favor!
- Failure, my God is the God of another chance!
- Sin, my God is a forgiver!
- Addiction, my God is a bondage breaker!
- Poverty, my God is rich!
- Weakness, my God is strong!

And finally, to everyone who has already dug your grave and written your obituary, simply because they see the fragmented pieces of your life, or the dry bones of your hopes and dreams scattered all over the place... declare, MY GOD IS A BONE COLLECTOR!

That's right... He's a bone collector! And He's collecting the pieces that are scattered and fragmented and causing them to come back together. He's causing the dead things to stand up. He's causing the pieces that looked beyond repair to become restored. He's causing everything that has been stolen to be returned. He's causing that which has held you in bondage to lose its grip. Child of God, watch what happens to your life when you not only speak to your mountain, but when you speak to your mountain about your God!

PRINCIPLE SIX
Speak through to the finish line

Now pay attention, because you need to hear this! Ezekiel spoke to the dry bones and verse 7-8 says:

> *So I prophesied as I was commanded; and as I prophesied, there was a noise, and suddenly a rattling; and the bones came together, bone to bone. Indeed, as I looked, the sinews and the flesh came upon them, and the skin covered them over...*
> **Ezekiel 37:7-8**

As Ezekiel began to speak what God said...as he began to speak up when he was tempted to shut up...as he began to talk to the dry bones, instead of about the dry bones... and as he spoke to his mountain about his God... sure enough, things began to change piece by piece!

First, there was noise. When you speak the right things over your life, the first thing that happens is the atmosphere around you changes. It becomes an atmosphere of faith and expectancy which becomes the breeding ground for miracles.

Second, God begins to put structures in your life; those are the bones standing up. God begins to give you foundations to build upon, so that the blessings He wants to add to your life have something to hang onto, and don't just collapse upon themselves.

Then God begins to add the blessings: the sinews, the flesh and the skin come on.

When you speak, God begins to bring things into divine order in your life. Little by slow, here a bit, there a bit, things start looking good.

You start to experience Jubilee, but then...

...*there was no breath in them.*

What does that mean? It means things begin to come into order, but the job has not been finished.

It's what often happens when we see life begin to come into order. We stop doing what we were doing to get to where we are. Circumstances are looking up, we get distracted by other things, and we let our confession slip.

But look at what God says in Ezekiel 37:9:

> *Also He said to me, "Prophesy to the breath, prophesy, son of man, and say to the breath, 'Thus says the Lord God: "Come from the four winds, O breath, and breathe on these slain, that they may live."'"*

What's the word of the Lord to you? Speak your promises through to the finish line. Don't stop speaking the Word over your life or declaring God's best. Don't stop, simply because it's getter better than it was…'cause God's not finished! Don't stop because the pain has become more manageable. Don't stop because you and your spouse had one night without an argument. Don't stop after you've lost five pounds. Don't stop because you got a raise. Don't stop because you slept through the night for the first time in months. Don't stop because you felt peaceful for a day. Don't stop because you finally paid the bills on time. Don't stop because your kid got saved.

Just don't stop! Remember nothing happens till you speak. So, speak it through till:

- you're so blessed you can't contain it
- you're so peaceful, they wonder if you've got a pulse
- you and your spouse start acting like newlyweds
- your child becomes a leader in the church
- you're so prosperous, you start blessing other people
- your life insurance goes down because you are so healthy

Speak it through to the finish line… speak it past the finish line… and then, keep on speaking it!

PRINCIPLE SEVEN
What you speak will change your circumstances

Remember Israel is scattered, fragmented and without hope. Their situation seems beyond repair. But God gives Ezekiel a strategy, and the strategy is simply, 'prophesy to these dead bones'.

Here is how our text resolves:

> "Behold, O My people, I will open your graves and cause you to come up from your graves, and bring you into the land of Israel. Then you shall know that I am the Lord, when I have opened your graves, O My people, and brought you up from your graves. I will put My Spirit in you, and you shall live, and I will place you in

your own land. Then you shall know that I, the Lord, have spoken it and performed it," says the Lord.'"

Look closely at what it says:

Verse 12: I **will open**...

Verse 13: you **shall know**... when I **have opened**...

Verse 14: I **will put**...; you **shall live**...; and I **will place**. Then you **shall know** that I, the Lord, **have spoken it and performed it.**

Do you notice the language? It's definitive, absolute. It's not a 'maybe'. It's not a 'might happen'. It's not, 'it's got a good chance of working.'

It is an absolute certainty. It's the words of Jesus in Mark 11 all over again. You WILL have what you say.

So say it!

Speak to your dry bones, Church, and they will live! Speak to your marriage; it will be restored! Speak to your body; it will be well. Speak to your finances; they will increase. Speak to your children; they will follow Jesus. Speak to your dreams; they will resurrect. Speak to what's been stolen; it will be returned. Speak to what's been broken; it will be restored.

Speak over your life. This is your banner year, and it will be the best year you ever had!

THIS IS MY YEAR OF JUBILEE

This is my year of victory!

This is my year of God's favor!

This is my year of good breaks!

This is my year the tide turns in my favor!

This is my year of increase!

This is my year of good health!

This is my year of seeing God show up in miracles!

This is my year to be set free!

This is my year of divine appointments & connections!

Shout it out, Church!

THIS IS MY BANNER YEAR!

Made in the USA
Middletown, DE
02 April 2018